T0209729

Ask Angel Amy

A.A.A
I can tow you out of your misery

Volume 1

AMY PIERCE

BALBOA
PRESS

A DIVISION OF HAY HOUSE

Balboa Press books may be ordered through booksellers or by contacting:

Balboa Press
A Division of Hay House
1663 Liberty Drive
Bloomington, IN 47403
www.balboapress.com
1 (877) 407-4847

Because of the dynamic nature of the Internet, any web addresses or
links contained in this book may have changed since publication and
may no longer be valid. The views expressed in this work are solely those
of the author and do not necessarily reflect the views of the publisher,
and the publisher hereby disclaims any responsibility for them.

The author of this book does not dispense medical advice or prescribe the use
of any technique as a form of treatment for physical, emotional, or medical
problems without the advice of a physician, either directly or indirectly. The
intent of the author is only to offer information of a general nature to help
you in your quest for emotional and spiritual well-being. In the event you use
any of the information in this book for yourself, which is your constitutional
right, the author and the publisher assume no responsibility for your actions.

Any people depicted in stock imagery provided by Getty Images are
models, and such images are being used for illustrative purposes only.
Certain stock imagery © Getty Images.

Print information available on the last page.

ISBN: 978-1-9822-3190-3 (sc)
ISBN: 978-1-9822-3191-0 (hc)
ISBN: 978-1-9822-3199-6 (e)

Library of Congress Control Number: 2019910229

Balboa Press rev. date: 08/09/2019

Contents

Abundance

Most people think that having money means you are abundant. The word abundance means you have more than enough of something. It is not just about money.

Every person has abundance, not every person has enough money to do the things they want to do.

We all have an abundance of air to breath, there is an abundance of people on this planet. There is an abundance of water and food on this earth. There is an abundance of trees, grass, rock, blue sky, stars, animals, there is an abundance of all of these things and more. When it rains there is an abundance of raindrops that fall, when it snows there is an abundance of snowflakes that fall. There is an abundance of knowledge and information at our very fingertips. We all have an abundance of problems and there is also an abundance of solutions.

You speak an abundance amount of words in your abundant number of days here on earth.

Why do you think and feel you are not abundant?

We are so very abundant that we are overlooking the abundance we have because many people focus on their lack of money and think that it means they are not abundant.

Abundance does not mean money.

Wealth means money.

When you pray or ask for abundance you are stopping the flow of it because you are feeling you are not abundant because of your lack of money.

Understand that you are abundant even though you are lacking money. These are two separate issues.

You can be abundant in your lack of money. You abundantly lack money, but you are abundant regardless of your lack of money.

Stop asking for abundance because you already are. Feel into that.

Ask for what it is that you want the money for. Money is just the means to get the thing you are asking for.

Money is like the middle man. Let go of the middle man and ask for what you want and feel the energy of that.

Begin to change the way you ask for what you want.

You can say, what would it take for this or that to show up. Leave money out of the equation.

If you need money to pay your bills ask for that. Ask how am I going to pay this bill. Ask the universe to show you how you can pay your bills.

If you need money to fix your car or your home etc. ask for help to show up.

Ask for what you want and be clear on what you are asking for. When you ask for money you are usually coming from a place of not having enough money. That is a vibration of lack that you send out that gets returned to you.

As always it is your choice to change your words or not.

No one can make this choice for you.

What are you going to choose to do?

Angel Amy

Believe in yourself

When you can believe in yourself you can do anything your heart desires. It is your own belief in yourself that propels you to your next place of awareness.

When you believe in yourself you feel a positive feeling. When you don't believe in yourself you feel a negative feeling. It is your choice to either believe in yourself or not. No one can help you with this. When your belief in yourself is strong then there is no one who can take anything away from you. You are the only one who knows what is right for you. Hold onto your beliefs within yourself and don't allow anyone to take your beliefs away from you until you decide to change them.

We all change our beliefs as we grow. If you choose to change your beliefs about certain things then that is your choice. Change is always good but you need to be the one to change yourself. No one can make you change.

If you are in a good positive place then your beliefs are working for you. If you are finding yourself in a negative place or a place of struggle then you may want to look at your beliefs and make a change.

Always believe in yourself and others will be able to see that your beliefs are working for you.

Do you need to change your beliefs?

This is a change that only you can make.

What are you going to choose to do?

Angel Amy

Choice

Our free will here on earth is our ability to choose. That's it. We all have the ability to choose the choices we make.

We can choose to be positive or negative. It's a choice.

We make choices all day unaware of what is really going on. We create our own reality by the choices we make.

Each one of us has a choice to choose to go down a positive path or a negative path. No path is a wrong path, all choices we make that lead us down our paths are exactly where we need to go.

You can choose to see the positive in people or you can choose to see the negative in people. Both are choices we all make. We make these choices all day, every day. Whether in person or watching TV, we all make choices.

You can choose to see the positive in your experiences or you can choose to see the negative in them. You have free will to choose the choices you want. But all perceptions are the choice of the individual for the reality they each need to experience regardless of what anyone else thinks.

You can choose to think this world is messed up or you can choose to see that everyone here is having their own unique experience for their own soul's growth. Whatever you choose, that is your free will. Choose what you want.

When you make your choices during your day choose from your heart and not your mind. Your heart will lead you down a positive path, your head may lead you down a negative path or a more safe path but there is no growth in being safe. The heart choice comes from a place of love, the head choice comes from ego. Again, no path is wrong, they are your choices but ask yourself how you want to feel every day.

The choices you make during your days need to come from you and not the influence of other people. There will always be someone out there who has a different opinion of your choices. We can't please everyone but we must begin to please ourselves.

Own your choices. Be proud of your choices. They are the unique expression of yourself.

This is your choice to make.

What are you going to choose to do?

Angel Amy

Dark

Dark is the opposite of Light.

The word Dark has an energy to it that only the individual can feel. Such is the same as with the word Light.

When you say the word light what do you feel? You feel light, high, bright, a sense of lightness, it just feels good.

When you say the word dark what do you feel? You feel heavy, dense, low, a sense of darkness, most of the time it doesn't feel good.

That is the difference between dark and light.

What you feel beyond that is what you attach your meaning of the words to. The words are what they are. That's it.

If you feel that something dark has any power over you then you need to understand that you are the one creating whatever it is you feel and your feelings are what attracts more of that into your reality.

Darkness has no power. You the individual gives power to the dark.

When you judge the meaning of this word you allow it to be bigger than yourself. It can only be bigger than yourself by allowing it, by thinking it has power over you. When you give darkness power over yourself you make yourself small and by doing this you make dark bigger, bigger than yourself.

You attach a feeling/emotion to the word and you give it life. By giving it life you are allowing it to destroy yourself.

Nothing has power over you unless you allow it.

Whatever you allow is your choice.

Some people don't want to wake up and see what is really going on and that is their choice to do so.

Some people do want to wake up and see what is really going on and that is their choice as well.

Neither choice is wrong, but you do need to make a choice.

Are you going to allow the dark to have control over you?

Are you going to choose to let darkness have power over you or can you now see it as being the opposite of light and that thought has no power?

The choice is yours to make.

What are you going to choose to do?

Angel Amy

Emotional Pain

When something happens to you that you don't like and causes you pain it is always the amount of intensity that you put on what you see that causes the pain you feel.

The lighter you can be in your moments when something goes the wrong way the less pain you will feel. Detach from the emotion when something does not go the way you want it to and you will feel more of a positive emotion rather than a negative one.

The reason you feel pain in the first place is because something has happened that you don't like. But if you can switch your awareness to a place of acceptance instead of disappointment then you will feel lighter. When there is something you have that means a great deal to you and it is taken away from you, you feel the emotion as being heavy and negative. If you can give that thing less emotion and have it not mean so much to you then you wouldn't feel as bad.

The negative feelings always come from the importance you put on whatever it is that you are focused on at that time.

Change your perception of what happens to you. See if from another angle and you will be able to change the emotion you are feeling.

Turn your negative emotions into love and acceptance for whatever is going on and you will begin to feel better.

Ask yourself what is this emotion trying to tell me, what can I learn here.

If you continue to carry negative emotions within your being you will find the reflection of that emotion in your reality. The emotion will continue until you can finally deal with it.

Accept the flow of life. Nothing is ever permanent. Things are always changing. Go with the flow of life and do not put so much importance on the material things that truly do not matter.

What really matters to each and every one of us is the feeling of love that we all carry within our hearts.

Tap into your own heart when things do not go the way you think they should and find the love and acceptance for the life you are living. The positive feeling is what we are all searching for. We all have it. We just have to find it within ourselves.

Example:

Driving in your car. Someone does something that you don't like, whether it be someone cutting you off, tailgating you, driving too fast, not using their blinker, etc. etc. Whatever happens when you are driving that bothers you is an emotion you are carrying with you. Your reality is reflecting it back to you because it is what you are carrying within your being. You are carrying an emotion that needs to be released.

Do the work to release it. Acknowledge, Accept, Allow yourself to feel the emotion and tell yourself you love yourself and it's ok to feel this. Take time to sit with this. This allows the negative feeling to be released.

As always this is something that only you can do.

What are you going to choose to do?

Angel Amy

Expectations

No one ever hurts your feelings. It is always your expectation of others that hurts your feelings.

When you expect someone else to treat you the way you expect to be treated you are setting yourself up to be hurt. Another person is another person. They have their own idea of how they are going to treat you.

Many times people have good relationships and there are never any issues but when you do have an issue with someone, anyone, it is only because you expected them to treat you how you wanted to be treated. Sometimes they cannot measure up to those expectations that you hold within yourself. This is where the phrase of a broken heart comes from. You think another person can break your heart by their words and actions.

No one can break another person's heart. Hearts cannot be broken. They can be "broken open" but never broken. The pain you feel when someone hurts you is your heart breaking open. The human body is not familiar with the heart being open which is why it feels painful. It feels painful because we are more familiar with our hearts being closed.

You feel pain because you think another person has hurt you but it is your very own expectation of others that has hurt you. You are the only one that can truly ever love yourself, you are the only one who can treat yourself how you want to be treated, that is not the job of another person.

We have all been taught that it is the job of others but it is not. You are here to love and accept yourself and allow others to have their own opinions and thoughts without judging them.

Do not expect others to always be there for you until you have already shown yourself that you are the one that is there for yourself first. When you show up for yourself there will be no need for you to keep expecting others to treat you a certain way, you will then be able to allow the opinions and thoughts of others to flow with no judgment of them.

Can you stop holding other people responsible for your happiness?

Can you understand that your expectations of others is the only thing that hurts you?

Can you allow others to have their own opinions and thoughts?

Can you stop expecting others to fulfill yourself?

This is a choice that only the individual can make.

Are you ready to make a choice to better serve yourself?

What are you going to choose to do?

Angel Amy

Failure

There is nothing any of us fail at. The word failure is part of the 3D paradigm. Society teaches failure. It is the opposite of achieving. Earth is made up of polarities, you can't have one end of the spectrum without the other end.

From a higher perspective there is no failure. All that is seen from a higher perspective is the experience. You the human turns your experiences into failure or achievement. Your higher self sees the experience and does not judge it as you do here on earth.

When you try to do something and you think you "fail" the only reason behind that is that it is not time for you to achieve whatever it is you are trying to achieve. You have something to learn by not achieving it. What you may be learning is perseverance, patience or love. You can never "fail" if you are always moving, always taking action, always seeing things as something other than "failure".

If you can view your "failures" as experiences then you take out "failing". You can't fail if you are having an experience. Change your awareness from what you have been taught by society and start seeing everything as an experiences.

Everyone is always doing the best they can with what they know.

Sometimes parents tell their children what to do and be. When a child is trying to do what the parents want them to do they find they cannot meet the expectations of the parent. This is seen as failure because the child did not come here to live the life of the parent or what the parent wants them to do. Children come here to have their own experiences but are not able to do so because the parents want them to do what they want the child to do.

Example:

If you are a parent you most likely want your child/ children to have what you never had. If you wanted to go to college but were unable to go for whatever reason, then you are going to want your child/children to go to college, because you think they need a good education to survive in this world. That is your belief from what you have learned here. So you make your Child go to college and what happens, they do not meet your expectations. They are not into learning because they are living your life and now getting low grades and this is now seen as a child failing. It is not failing. Every child that comes here to earth has their own thoughts and desires of what they want to do. When a child is forced to live their lives the way the parents want them to then they will not thrive. They continue living what their parents want so they can finally make the parents proud, even though they have dreams that they have had to squash down within themselves. This is also the root cause of illnesses.

If you want your children the thrive allow them to be who it is they came here to be. Allow them their own experiences regardless of what happens. Everything is just an experience if you can take the word "failure" out of your vocabulary.

No one ever "fails". You can think you "fail" but you never really "fail". You have an experience, that's it.

Allow your children to fulfill their own dreams and they will thrive. It is only when they are living their lives in a way they think someone else wants them to live that it is seen as "failure" if they aren't meeting the expectations of someone else.

When you live your life the way someone else wants you to live it you are not living, you will not thrive. We thrive when we are able to live our lives the way we each want to live it regardless of what anyone says.

It's time to break free of the expectations of others and live our lives the way we are meant to. The only way to do this is to listen to our own inner being.

You are the only one who can choose what you want to do.

You are the only one who can choose to let go of your children living your life.

You are the only one who can stop expecting others to prove something to you.

What are you going to choose to do?

Angel Amy

FEAR
- False Evidence/Energy Appearing Real

Fear is one of the illusions we have in this reality. It is an illusion. It cannot hurt you. Only your thoughts and beliefs hurt you.

Fear shows up when you do not trust yourself and when you do not believe in yourself.

When you allow fear to control your actions you give up your own control, you give up your own personal power and you hand it over to this feeling you have.

Fear is not you. It is not something that you are. It's like a program that you have bought into. A belief that you are carrying that says you can't, shouldn't, you aren't worthy, etc. etc.

When something shows up that you truly want to do and you suddenly feel fear because the mind pops in and comes up with all the reasons you can't or shouldn't do what it is you want, notice what happens. You have an idea first of what you want but then the mind jumps in.

These are two aspects of you but you have to be able to understand the two aspects are different. They are not the same energy. One feels positive and one feels negative/resistance.

Don't squash it down inside yourself, don't brush it aside, this will only keep it alive only to be repeated later on in life.

When you feel fear acknowledge it, sit with the feeling and allow it to come up, allow it to be there then wait for it to leave.

Fear is just your ego's way of keeping you safe. Being safe does not move you forward and it doesn't allow you to live your life to the fullest.

We did not come to earth to play it safe, we came to earth to experience, expand and grow. You only grow when you deal with your fears and then work through them.

As always, this is your choice to choose what you want to do.

What are you going to do?

Angel Amy

The Game

This is a concept that is very hard to understand only because of the intensity of it.

Life is a Game. You have a choice to allow yourself to play the game or be played by the game. Until you wake up to an understanding of the Game you will be played by the game.

The intensity of pain on this planet is what makes it hard to believe in this game.

One will argue that the pain a person endures cannot be considered a game at all. This was also my thinking until I did the research.

I found out that we all choose our realities. We all choose what it is we want to experience here on earth. I found out that our choices we make down here create our reality. I found out that we make our choices before we come to this reality, we make our choices from a perception of being in a blissful state.

I found out that this is the biggest game in the universe and nothing has or ever can go wrong with anything here on earth.

The mind will tell us otherwise. The mind will try to keep us safe and protected from everything. The mind does not want us to advance because the mind is in fear. The mind does not know what is really going on, it's not programmed to know, it is programmed to think, thinking for the human is the job of the mind.

I encourage everyone to do their own research, make your own judgments and listen to your own heart.

But what I learned from my research has given me the clarity I needed to perceive what we call reality. It's not what we think. There are reasons for everything and it all makes so much sense to me now. I understand the concept of this game that we all play. It is a game and when you understand the game you are more able to play it rather than having the game play you.

We don't know what we don't know. When you finally wake up and understand how things work it makes this life we all live a much more fulfilling place to be in.

Understanding is the key to your perception. Your perception creates your reality. Your reality can be either painful, confusing, difficult, useless, unrewarding, unfulfilling and downright nasty or it can be the most rewarding, exciting, fulfilling, beautiful and heartfelt place to be. You are the decider of your perception. The mind will tell you everything has gone wrong but your heart will understand nothing can go wrong.

The books I recommend to anyone wanting to understand why we are here are:

Journey of Souls by Michael Newton PH.D.

Delores Cannon books or You Tube Videos

Busting loose from the Business Game or Busting loose from the Money Game By Robert Scheinfeld

Do your own research and see what you think for yourself. Open your mind and be willing to see things differently.

Life is a game.

Are you going to play the game or are you going to let the game play you?

The choice is yours.

Only you can choose what you want to do.

What are you going to choose to do?

Angel Amy

Heartbroken

Your heart may feel like it is breaking but it can never be broken. The human heart is not breakable.

When your heart feels pain it is not that it is breaking, it's that it is breaking opening.

What the human does not understand is the pain you feel when someone hurts you is nothing more than your human muscle of the heart. It hurts so bad because we are human and we are not aware of the depth of the feeling of love just yet.

It's like when you go to work out and the next day your muscles hurt. It's only because you haven't used those muscles and that is why you feel pain. The body is merely adjusting to the muscle that is being used. It's the same with the heart.

The average human does not love on a deep level most of the time. We love but the love we are capable of feeling isn't something most people have discovered just yet.

True love here on earth is very deep. When you connect with someone on a deep level your love for them is intense. It goes beyond words and can only be described within the human that possess that feeling. This feeling is an act of the heart opening, not breaking, but breaking open.

The people you have lost have been a catalyst for you to open your heart, why, because their life path mingles with your life purpose. They chose to be in your life to help you open your heart. You chose to be in their life to be inspired by the life they had lived. If you can remember this the next time a loved one leaves you then you will be starting to see the purpose and the connection in both of your lives.

Your life has purpose and everyone else's life has a purpose. Understanding the purpose is something that needs to be discovered by the individual.

Be willing to open your heart whenever you can, whenever an opportunity for it arises.

Crying doesn't always mean sad and hurt. Crying is a release and at the same time it is an opening up of the heart. Cry all you want when you feel the need to. But do not associate crying with heartbreak. Crying is you opening your heart and connecting with your inner self. When you cry your human aspect does not understand that it has made a connection with the inner self.

You are not heartbroken, you are beginning to open your heart on a level that you are not aware of.

What you do with your heart is your business.

What you allow in to your consciousness is also your business.

Teaching the meaning of heartbreak is my business.

What you choose to do is always your business.

What are you going to choose to do?

Angel Amy

Influence your own thoughts

When you have a thought that does not serve you stop and ask yourself who's thought is this? Is this really my own thought or did it perhaps come from someone else?

Everything we have been taught has been taught to us by someone else. Someone else that has a different upbringing than us, someone with many different life experiences than ourselves. People who teach are usually trying to get others to think what they believe. This goes for little things just as much as the big things in our lives.

I would like to teach you to think for yourself. Make your own choices in life so that you can take responsibility for yourself, so you don't blame someone else because you did something they taught you to do only to find out if didn't work for you.

It's time to choose for yourself. Make choices that influence your own heart.

Make your own choices when it comes to your life choices such as going to school, buying a new home or renting one, purchasing a new car, coloring your hair, wearing clothes that are in style or what to eat. All these things are things that you can choose for yourself.

If you want/have been inspired to go to school then do so, take the steps to begin that process but do it because you truly want it for yourself and not because someone else is telling you that is what you should do.

If you are in the market to purchase a new home, make sure it's what you want to do instead of renting a new home. You need to make the right decision for yourself. What feels right to you?

Instead of looking at the comments about a car trust your instincts. Don't listen to someone tell you that the brand that you love doesn't have good gas mileage or isn't a good car for whatever reason. The car you fall in love with will serve you. The car you buy because of others opinions will not serve you, it serves the other person but the other person is not the one buying the car. Listen to your heart and get the car that you will be happy with regardless of someone else's opinion.

Many people today are coloring their hair all kinds of colors. Why, because they are exercising their free will to do so, they can and they don't care what anyone else thinks. They are not asking for anyone's approval they are expressing themselves. That is freedom. Freedom to choose for yourself.

The style of clothing changes all the time. I never buy cloths because of whether it is in style or not, I buy clothes for the way they make me feel. If I don't like the style that is out I just don't buy them and I don't care what anyone thinks. We all have the right to wear what we want. Stop letting society dictate what you should wear and choose to wear what makes you feel good.

Everyone has an opinion on what we should be eating. If you are overweight and want to lose the weight then yes you have to find what will work for you in order for you to lose the weight. But with that you too have to find the right program that works for you. Not every program will work for you. Listen to what is right for you.

If you enjoy eating then you should enjoy the food that you want to eat. If you are enjoying your food then that is all that should matter. If you want to eat healthy, then eat healthy but not everything healthy is good for everyone. Some people cannot eat the healthy organic items that are out now. You have to choose for yourself.

Begin to listen to your own inner being when you want to do anything. What is good for one person may not be good for another person. Begin to influence your own thoughts.

You are the only one that can make choices for yourself.

What are you going to choose to do?

Angel Amy

Judgment

Judgment, Judgment, Judgment. We all do it all day every day. We judge everything. The way someone looks, the clothes we wear and what others wear, the color of a person's hair, how someone talks. etc, etc.

We judge all things that we see. We apply a human trait onto the things we see during our days. This is natural, it's human but it is not where we are going.

When we judge someone or something we are not understanding what is really going on. We are not understanding that life is about variety. Not everyone is going to like everything about everyone here.

Judgments come from each person's individual perception.

When you judge someone for how they look you are not understanding that they are not here to please you.

When you judge someone for how they live you are not understanding they are not you and they have different wants and needs in this lifetime along with a different path to follow.

When you judge someone for doing something you think is wrong you are not understanding they are doing the best they can with the knowledge they have.

When you judge someone you are not fully understanding there are many variations of beings on this planet and each and every one of them is individual and unique in their own way. No one is here to please you, everyone is here to express their individuality.

Judgment comes from the mind, it does not come from the heart. When you operate from the mind during your day you are creating your life from the ego perception. When you open up and come from the heart during your day you are creating your life from a place of love. Neither place is right or wrong but when you come from the mind it keeps you trapped in a lower vibrational place that has no growth. When you come from the heart you are accepting things on a higher level of perception and it will bring out the love you have inside yourself.

You are the only one who can decide where you want to come from. It is a choice that is made unconsciously every day by everyone until you wake up and become conscious of the choices you are making every day.

You are the only one who can choose those thoughts for yourself.

What are you going to choose to do?

Angel Amy

Knowing

We all have an inner knowing. It's a deep down inner knowing. We need to begin going there when making decisions. Have you ever said to yourself "deep down" I knew that would happen or "deep down" I knew it wouldn't happen. We need to tap into "deep down" more often. Listen to your inner knowing about the choices you make, listen "deep down" for your answers, they are there but most times we listen to the ego off the top of our heads.

Deep down is where our intuition is. Deep down is our inner knowing but we are so used to listening from the place of the ego that we don't always hear the "deep down" answers.

Start paying attention to your "deep down". Once you start listening there you will find it gets easier to listen to and soon you will be coming from the "deep down" place all the time.

Be aware of where you are when making decisions and choices. Where are your thoughts, take a minute and come from the "deep down" within yourself.

Your inner knowing, the "deep down" is always there trying to get your attention.

You can choose to go "deep down" or you can continue to listen to the ego.

The choice is yours and yours alone to make.

What are you going to choose to do?

Angel Amy

Listen to your own heart

Whenever you are faced with a decision about something you are wanting to do or to purchase stop and feel where you are coming from when making that decision.

Some people look at the statistics in order to make their decisions. These statistics have been based upon polls taken by others. When you make your decisions based on this you need to understand you are giving away your power to others.

When you listen to what someone else has given their opinion on, you are neglecting your own opinion. You are listening with you mind and not your heart.

It's time to start listening to your own heart and not the minds of others.

You are not other people, you have your own thoughts and ideas about things. You have your own wants and needs. You are the only one who can choose what is right for you and you do this by listening to your very own heart.

A good example is buying a car. When you are in the market for purchasing a car for yourself all you need to do is listen to your heart. Which car gets you excited and feels good to you, which one do you love? Go with that feeling and don't listen to what the paperwork says. Let go of the statistics that are written out. Just feel with your heart and things will magically work out for you.

We all try to buy the best thing for us, whatever that is, a car, a house, food, a book or any other item we want. We analyze it through other people's opinions.

The next time you are making a purchase, big or small, listen to your heart. Pay attention to what feels right to you.

The only thing we really ever need to do when making a purchase is to listen to our own feelings. That is not always easy to do because there is always someone there to talk ourselves out of the thing that makes our hearts sing.

The choice is always yours to make.

You can choose to listen to others or you can choose to listen to yourself.

What are you going to choose to do?

Angel Amy

Money

We have allowed money to control us far too long. We think money is the answer to everything. We think once we have money we can finally be happy.

Happiness doesn't come from money. True happiness comes from within your very own being. True happiness is an inside job.

We all want money because we think it will make us feel better. The feeling everyone is looking for comes from within us, it doesn't come from money.

Money can buy a lot of things but the things that really matter cannot be purchased. What truly matters is love and how you give to yourself and others.

All anyone really wants is a feeling. A feeling of love, excitement, joy, freedom. Those things cannot be bought, they need to felt with the heart.

If you insist that you want money and you think money will make you happy stop and ask yourself, what is it that I want the money for.

Do you want money because you want to feel freedom from paying your bills?
Do you want money because you want to stop feeling you are living a poverty lifestyle?
Do you want money because you want the feeling of being secure?
Do you want money because you think it can buy you the things that will make you happy?

What you truly want is a feeling. A feeling that is within you, it's just been hidden because we have been taught to strive for money in order to get ahead in this world.

Money can't buy happiness. Once you have money for the thing you thought you wanted it for, the thing you thought would make you happy, something else will show up for you to want to be happy about. It just continues to grow and you continue to want to find happiness.

Tap into your feelings of self worth if you want to attract money into your life. Find your own self worth, that is where money comes from.

Start to appreciate the things you do have in your life. When you only look at the things you want money for you are neglecting what you already do have. Look at the things in your reality that you do have, write them down so you can see more clearly what you have. Appreciate those things that you do have and that feeling will begin to open you up to more coming in.

Money only rules this world when we think it does. It really doesn't. Love rules the world but not everyone can see that. Love is the emotion that everyone is trying to find. You can find it by appreciating what you already have.

You are the only one that can tap into the emotion of love to find true happiness.

It is a choice only you can make.

What are you going to choose to do?

Angel Amy

New Earth and the Old Earth

The old earth is the 3rd dimension. The old earth is where we play out our reality in a very dense way. We can only see and feel the density of the limitations that are there. It is where we play out certain cycles that we learn to let go of. It is a playground for the human aspects of ourselves to choose to either stay there playing in it or to begin to move out of it. We are not meant to stay in one particular dimension, we are meant to experience, grow and expand as we move through the dimensions here on earth.

The new earth is the 5th Dimension. But it is not limited to just the 5th, this is just the next Dimension available to us as we grow and expand our awareness. The possibilities are endless as we keep moving forward. The only thing that ever slows us down is our perception of who we are.

We are multi-Dimensional beings that came to this earth to experience, expand and continue to grow. We can only do this if we let go of our limited thinking that keeps us in a lower place.

With each dimension comes a feeling. This feeling determines your vibrational state of where you are. The higher the dimension the better feeling you are able to access. This is when you raise your vibration.

The choices and decisions that you make will determine the dimension you choose to be in.

No dimension is right or wrong, they are just different and can only be stepped into by the perception of the individual.

As always the decision is always yours to make.

What are you going to choose to do?

Angel Amy

Over thinking your experiences

There is always something else going on. If we can stop over thinking things we would be able to see what is really happening.

Whenever you stop and think that something is not right with a situation or circumstance be aware that it may not be what you think.

If a family member or friend seems off to you, don't think that it's you. They could be going through something that they aren't yet ready to share.

There is always something else going on in this reality.

When buying a car, it's not really about just buying a car, it's about your physical vehicle readjusting to a new vibration.

When buying or renting a new home, it's not about just buying or renting a new home, it's about you being called to return home, within your heart.

When you download a program or app on your phone, it's not just about what you are doing, it's about your physical body getting downloads of energy.

When your cell phone is always running low on battery, it's not just about your cell phone, it's about your physical body running low on energy.

When you continue to get phone calls that you think are from no one, those phone calls represent someone from the other side trying to get in touch with you.

When you see an animal in your path, it's not by chance that an animal has crossed your path. Animals carry messages. Look up what the meaning of that certain animal is, look online and see what it is. Dead animals have just as much meaning as live ones do.

When an appointment gets changed, don't get frustrated, see it in a different way, see it as maybe there is a reason for the change, maybe there is someone you are suppose to meet on the new day, you don't know but when you allow life to show you how it works that is when the magic happens.

When you forget something in a grocery store there is a reason you forgot it. As you go back in to the store maybe there will be someone you need to see, even if you don't understand the reason, you never know what is going on but there is always a reason for it. Maybe you needed to smile at someone who needed a smile that very minute they saw you.

When something happens to you and the circumstances are such that you need to make another trip to a certain place, it's not that the thing went wrong, it's just the universe's way of saying you need to go back to that place another day. You don't need to know why, you just need to understand that you don't know the reason for this thing that is happening and all you have to do is to allow it.

The reasons that things happen don't always have to be big, they can be the smallest of reasons but they all matter. You don't need to understand why they matter, you need to understand that they do.

When you begin to live your life with this awareness you will find life just gets easier for you. It will begin to flow and magic will happen.

Stop over thinking what happens during your day and begin to understand the language of the universe and your life will flow more easily for you.

As you pay attention to the circumstances during your day this is how you play the game and you begin to stop the game from playing you.

As always it is your choice to play this game or not.

You get to choose for yourself.

What are you going to choose to do?

Angel Amy

Perception

Your perception is what you perceive. Another person's perception is what they perceive. No perception is right and no perception is wrong. They are just what the individual sees.

With so many humans here on this planet we must understand that there are that many perceptions being perceived.

What one person thinks as being right another person may perceive as being wrong.

Both are relevant. Both are valuable. Both are correct for the individual.

If one person wants to eat a certain way they should be able to do so. If another person wants to eat a different way they too should be able to do so.

Perception is about viewing reality the way the individual sees it.

Each person has their own perception of how they see life. We are all different and we all have our own perception of how we should live our lives and how we want it to be.

If we can remember during our days that we all have a different perception of life then we would be living in a world of love. We would be coming from a place of love and not fear.

Your perception comes from your life experiences. Another person's perception comes from their life experiences. No two are the same. Each and every one of us come from a different state of being, a different place of upbringing. Each one of us is here to experience different things.

It is the individual perception of the person that dictates how that person's reality will be played out. Again, no right or wrong here. Each person's perception is just that, their own perception, how they view the world.

Perception is an individual state of consciousness.

Only the individual can choose how to perceive the world.

As always it is your choice to choose what you want to do.

How are you going to perceive your world?

What are you going to choose?

Angel Amy

Quit

I Quit, I quit playing this 3rd dimensional reality. I quit.

I quit being the victim and start seeing that the experiences where I felt like a victim were parts of my reality that were helping me to grow. When I felt like a victim it was me giving my power away and with that understanding I step out of the victim role I was playing.

I quit seeing life through my eyes that had blinders on. I now see clearly that I agreed to go through everything that I have gone through. I understand I had my guidance team on the other side helping me with my decisions before I came into this reality.

I quit blaming others. I now understand there is never anyone to blame because I am the one who chose to have the experiences that I have had. I chose them before I came into this reality.

I quit feeling guilty for the things I have done that I thought were wrong. Nothing is ever wrong, all experiences are just that, experiences that I chose to have in order for my soul to grow.

I quit thinking the human me is in charge. I am not in charge, my soul is in charge and when I understand this I let go of trying to control my life. The harder I tried to control my life the more frustrated I got with life. Once I let go of trying to control things that is when life began to fall into place. Things would just work out for me. I let go and the magic began.

I quit seeing this world as ugly and horrible. I now am able to see the beauty in every day regardless of what happens. We don't understand what we don't know. I have learned that when my soul leaves this body here and crosses over into the spirit world that it has no form, there is no human vehicle to hold it, which means being here in the physical is very meaningful. We get to eat, drink, smell, taste, touch, feel and think. We need the physical body in order to feel the sensation, we don't feel the sensation in the spirit world.

I quit trying to change others and saw that they are here having their own life experience and I saw clearly that their life was very different from mine. Everyone has a different perception of things.

I quit listening to society tell me what to do. We have been trained to listen to others. It's time to begin listening to our own thoughts and feelings. Society tells us that we need 8 hours of sleep every day. Not everyone is able to get 8 hours of sleep every day and when we don't then we think there is something wrong because we have been taught we need that much sleep. I now tell myself that even though I only got 6 hours of sleep my body will function as it should. Funny thing is that this always works for me.

Society tells us that breakfast is the most important meal of the day. I quit listening to that one too. I eat when I am hungry and my body operates just fine.

Society tells us that we need 8 glasses of water a day. I now listen to my body and when I feel thirsty then I have the water. My body knows what it is doing, all I have to do is listen to it and not to society.

Quit listening to society and take back your power and begin to listen to yourself.

As always, this is a choice that only you can make for yourself.

What are you going to choose to do?

Angel Amy

Respond or React

Our free will here on earth is our choice to choose. We choose to either respond or react. That's it. With every situation that arises you have a choice to respond or react. How you respond and how you react are very important to the outcome of what it is that is going on.

When you respond you are coming from your heart.

When you react you are coming from your ego/mind.

When you can respond you are coming from a place of peace within yourself. A response doesn't carry any negative emotion with it.

When you react you are coming from a place of being triggered. Triggers carry negative emotions that are held within your being that need to be released.

Pay attention to yourself the next time you respond or react to something. Feel the difference so you can begin to determine what is going on with yourself. If you find yourself reacting more than you are responding then listen to that and ask yourself why you are reacting, what emotions you are holding onto that need to be released.

Only you can choose to listen to yourself.

What are you going to choose to do?

Angel Amy

Sleep

How much sleep do you need?
The answer is: It is different for everyone.

Some people need very little and others require more.
There is no one answer that fits everyone. Society tells
us that we should get 8 hours of sleep each night. So
when a person doesn't get the 8 hours that society says
they should get they think there is something wrong
with them, they try to figure out why they can't get
8 hours. This 8 hours of sleep requirement is not for
everyone and it causes people to think they are doing
something wrong.

You need what you need. That's it.

Stop letting society dictate what is right for you. You
are the only one who knows what is right for you.

Begin to tell your mind that you get the appropriate amount of sleep for yourself.

Some people need more down time than others. When your body sleeps your soul goes out. Your soul is on the other side while you are sleeping. Your soul may be conversing with your guides and getting information for your next steps to take here on earth. Your soul may be traveling somewhere else, the soul does not need sleep but the human does.

There is more energy coming in now than ever before and sometimes you need to sleep in order for your body to receive the energy. That is usually why a person may feel the need to take a nap during the day, their bodies are being "worked on". Doesn't it feel better to say your body is being worked on rather than thinking there is something wrong with you if you feel you need to take a nap?

The human needs to rest but the spirit does not. The human body is constantly changing even though we cannot see it. Allow the changes to integrate within your body and sleep when you feel the need to sleep as long as you are able to do so.

Don't ever think there is anything wrong with you because of the number of hours you sleep or don't sleep. We are all individual and we all require different amounts of sleep regardless of what society tell us.

You are in charge of your body.

Only you make decisions for your body.

What are you going to choose to do?

Angel Amy

Triggers

When you get triggered by someone or something the bottom line message is always about you and not the other person or thing.

Emotional triggers happen when you are not in alignment with your soul. Triggers show up as an emotion within you to let you know that you are out of alignment.

The reason for a trigger is always because you are holding onto an old emotion that you have not dealt with and you think it is the doing of another person that makes an emotion come up and you end up giving your power to someone or something outside of yourself.

Other people show up to trigger us because they are there to be the reflection of us. They are merely responding to the law of attraction. You have attracted them into your life because you both operating at the same vibration. The emotions that you hold inside of yourself are what will appear outside of yourself. Emotions are magnetic.

When you get triggered stop and ask yourself why are you not loving yourself in this moment. Why is it that you have given your power to someone or something outside of yourself?

Where can you begin to love yourself more? What can you now see that you can let go of in order to stop this trigger from repeating.

Ask for guidance when you get triggered. Ask for help so you can see where you are not loving yourself enough.

As Always this is your choice to do or not.

What are you going to choose to do?

Angel Amy

Understanding

When you understand you don't judge. When you judge you are not understanding.

If we all could begin to understand life a little more this world would be a better place for us to live.

Everyone has their own ideas about this life we live and we all judge the way we see things.

It's time we all begin to understand we are one piece of the puzzle here on earth. With each human being here on earth there is a different aspect of self-expression.

We are individual for a reason. We each express our own individual expression of who we are. When we can understand this we can begin to allow others to express themselves however they choose to. We are not here to judge one another we are here to expand and grow. How can we grow if we stay the same, the same person we were last year, the same person we were 10 years ago. We all grow and change.

If you stay the same there is no growth in your life. If you stay the same you are not allowing your true inner expression to come out.

Understanding for ourselves and others is imperative if we want to continue to grow and expand. Understand that life is not meant to be the same, life itself will continue to change and grow regardless of how you view it.

Understand we are all individual.
Understand we all have different wants and needs.
Understand the way we each see another person is merely our individual perception.
Understand the way we treat others is really the way we treat ourselves.
Understand the good inside each of us is an expression of your inner being.
Understand the bad inside each of us is merely a negative emotion that has been pushed down inside the human aspect of the individual.
Understand that negative emotions need to be acknowledged and loved and not pushed aside.

The next time you judge something, the next time you condemn something, the next time criticize something stop and ask yourself, what am I not understanding about this.

We walk around here on earth not understanding the real reasons for what we see. We don't understand why some people want to color their hair a different color, we don't understand why people choose to wear the clothes they wear, no matter how freaky, unusual ......

We all have different reasons for doing the things we do. Try to understand there is a reason others do what they do. We don't have to know the reason, all we have to do is UNDERSTAND there is a reason.

Some people wear clothes that remind them of their loved ones who are no longer here. They don't care what it looks like all they care about is keeping the memory of their loved ones with them. It makes them feel good.

Some people tattoo their bodies. Can we all try and understand why a person puts a tattoo on their body. It's just a reflection of their insides, they want to show their creative aspect of themselves. They want to express what they feel inside themselves. Some want to honor their loved ones and put their name or a symbol of their loved ones on their body as to remember them. Some are tapping into their past lives of when they were Indians and wore paint on their bodies. It doesn't matter the reason, all that matters is they are expressing themselves in their own way. Not everyone likes tattoos but everyone should be allowed to get one if that is what they choose. We all should be able to understand that the only reason anyone gets a tattoo is because they have chosen to and that is their human free will to do.

Some people color their hair in blues, pinks, purples etc. Why because it's their free will to do what they want to do regardless of what anyone else thinks. It makes them feel good to change their hair color to whatever they want.

All anyone is ever trying to do in this reality is to make themselves feel good. What they choose to do with their bodies should be their choice. Understand this and you will be taking away the judgment of them.

If we could all apply just a little more understanding during our day we would feel a lot better.

It's time we move out of judging others and begin to understand we are all different and what one chooses to do with their body is their business. How one chooses to express themselves is their business. How one chooses to live is their business.

We are all here playing this earth game.

Understanding is one of the keys that we have to a better future.

Can you start your day with more understanding of others?
Can you look at someone and understand they are doing what they choose to do.
Can you look at a situation and understand it only the perception you are holding that makes it what it is.
Can you understand you are a spiritual being living within the human vessel?
Can you understand that you cannot make a wrong choice?
Can you understand that you make better choices when you are listening to your heart?

It is always your choice to understand or not.

You can apply understanding during your day or you can choose to close it off.

It is your choice.

What are you going to choose to do?

Angel Amy

Valentine's Day

Valentine's Day has been put into place by society, by others, by the old beliefs.

It's part of the earth game we play here. You are alive, so you have a choice to either play the game or not. When you choose to play the game then the game can no longer play you.

Take "Valentine's Day" and love, JUST LOVE. Make it about the awareness that you are able to love and that means starting with yourself. Begin loving yourself on this "Valentine's Day". You are the only one who can really love yourself.

Those who have partners will pay extra attention to their partners on this day because society has told them that is what this day is about. Why can't we always pay extra attention to our partners? Do we really need a special day to do that, do you really need to be reminded to love your partner. Hopefully if you have a partner that partner is special to you every day.

And if you don't have a partner then the message is very clear. Love yourself. You are all you have. No one outside of you can truly give yourself the love that you are searching for. Love is an inside job. Only you can do it.

Loving yourself is one of the greatest gifts we can give ourselves.

Love and appreciate the life you have chosen to live.

Be grateful for being alive. It has more meaning than you can comprehend.

Do you really need someone outside of yourself, like society, to tell you to love? It's time to get past society and what it dictate to us. Stop letting the game play you.

When you hold love in your heart then you are able to love every day, you don't need a special day to love.

The spirit inside each and every one of us is trying to come out and express itself. It is trying to express love, it can only express love if the human aspect of you can allow it.

We all have love in our hearts, we are all capable of loving. You can choose to be an expression of love EVERY DAY not just on "Valentine's Day".

These holidays have gotten extremely commercialized. It has turned into "what can you buy at the store"? You can't buy love from a store but society wants us to think it comes from a store. It doesn't. It's an expression of the heart.

The real meaning of Valentine's Day is love. Choose how you want to express that love regardless of what society tells us to do.

Choose to love every day!

The choice is yours to make, only the individual can choose what is right for them.

What are you going to choose to do?

Angel Amy

Working on it

There is never anything you need to work on in life. The only thing that needs working on is your judgment of what is going on. Work on letting go of judging the things that are happening to you. Work on forgiving and loving yourself. Those are the things that need working on not the things you are doing or trying to do.

If there is something in your life that you are wanting to do and you cannot see how you will be able to do/ accomplish it then stop and wait for the inspiration to come. It will, it will only be your judgment of it NOT coming that will frustrate you. Have some faith, have some confidence, have some understanding that things happen when you are open to them happening.

You cannot force life to do what you want it to do. The only way to get what you actually want is to be patient and allow the universe to bring it to you. It will.

Begin to understand how the universe works. When you continue to say I need to work on this, what the universe hears is, you need to work on this. That is what you are creating, more working on it. The universe does not judge, the universe delivers, do you understand?

If you think you need to work on being a better person/parent/friend/lover, don't go into feeling you need to work at it. Just begin, just be it, be aware of what you are doing and the choices you are making. If you think you are doing something wrong because you haven't been the best you can be at something, then thinking that thought takes you out of creating the person you do want to be.

Your judgment of your life is not accurate. We have been taught by society that we are not enough, that we are not good enough because of whatever it is that we have already done. This is not accurate. You have done the best you could with the knowledge that you already have within yourself. This doesn't mean you cannot expand and grow into being better, it just means you have to accept the person you are in order to continue to grow and move forward.

If you want to grow and move forward all you have to do is stop working so hard on your life and just allow it to happen. Shift your focus on the good things you have accomplished. Let go of the negative, they have been there to help guide you just as much as the positive.

Feel the energy of "I have to work on this" and then feel the energy when you let that thought go.

You are the only one who can change the things in your life. Begin with changing how you see your life. Begin by letting go of your judgment of the things you think you are doing wrong and begin to love yourself from deep within.

This is a journey we are all on here. A journey of self discovery. Nothing we have done in the past is wrong. The past is about experiences we needed to have in order for our souls to grow.

Just keep on discovering the person that is inside of this human vehicle. There is more to you than you are able to grasp at this moment.

As always, this is a choice only you can make.

A choice to stop working so hard on your life or continue to work hard on your life.

What are you going to choose to do?

Angel Amy

H

X marks the spot. The spot is exactly where you are now. It is exactly where you are on this journey.

X is where you are meant to be.
There is no way out of X.
X is your current moment and that is what you will be seeing even when you move forward.

Regardless of the turmoil, trauma, confusion, pain, joy, beauty, fun or excitement, you are where you need to be. There can be no other way.

Life does not make mistakes.

So if you are questioning where you are stop and ask yourself why do I think I am here in this X spot right now? What is this current experience trying to show me? There is always something to be seen in whatever it is you are going through other than what you think you are experiencing.

Choose to see your now X moment as a place you are meant to be so you can move forward into your next phase here on earth.

Choose to see your X moment as a place of growth, not on the physical level but on the spiritual level.

Choose to be at peace with your X moment and allow for change to happen.

You are the only one who can choose what you are going to do.

What are you going to choose to do?

Angel Amy

Yesterday is gone, or is it?

When you continue to think the same thoughts you thought yesterday what you are doing is bringing yesterday into the now.

We don't understand that each morning we wake up is a new day. It isn't yesterday. If we can all begin to tell ourselves new stories each day as we wake up then our reality would change. Our bodies are changing all the time. We have to bring the mind on board to begin to actually change our reality.

Do you wake up each morning thinking you are the same person as yesterday? You have the ability to change your yesterday story if you understand that today you are given another chance to change. Only you can do this. Only you can tap into the part of you that can change.

Allow the mind to come on board with the heart. The heart is open and waiting.

Example is: If you wake up and continue to think you cannot make any money doing what you are doing, or you can't make any money without this other thing in your life then you are just living your yesterday out all over again.

If you wake up and start telling yourself that money will find its way to you, even though you don't know how, that is what you will be creating.

This is how we create new.

Begin thinking new thoughts each and every day. Ask for guidance and help if you need it.

Start your next day telling yourself a new story and believe it. Believe it because you are it.

You can only move forward if you are willing to move forward and leave your past where it is meant to be, in the past.

Now means now, not yesterday. Stop bringing your yesterdays into the now and watch what happens.

You are the only one who can make this choice for yourself.

What are you going to choose to do?

Angel Amy

Zero

What do you get for being here on earth?
What do you get for going through the tough times?
What do you get for having to endure so much pain while here on earth?
What do you get for fighting your way through this reality?
What do you get?

You get Zero.

You get nothing, there is zero cost.

You gain wisdom, you gain clarity, you gain understanding and so much more but you get zero, you get nothing tangible for being here.

There is no reward for being good. Your mind will tell you there must be a reward for all this good hard work you have accomplished this lifetime, but there isn't any reward waiting for anyone who has been "good".

Each one of us is here of our own free will by choice regardless of whether or not you believe it.

Each one of us is living the life we chose. Being allowed to come into reality isn't about what we can get it's about what we experience and how we handle those experiences.

If you can understand that you chose to come here then try to see where in your reality you are expecting something in return. Do you find yourself saying, I did all this work here and this is what I get?

Do you find yourself saying to your children, I brought you into this world and brought you up and this is what I get?

Do you find yourself saying I did everything right and this is what I get?

If you say those statements you may want to change the way you see your reality.

Why is it that some people do their very best at working hard and get zero in return?

It's because we aren't here to do our best at working hard. We are here to experience life, all aspects of it, the good, the bad, the painful and the joyful. We aren't here to be "good". We are here to explore and experience. There is no good or bad in experience.

I am not saying we are here to be mean people. What I am saying is we are here to listen to our own hearts and do what is right for us and us alone. When you listen to your own heart you will find you are unable to be mean, you will find you become more loving to yourself and others. That is when your life will turn around and become the life you want instead of the life you are struggling in.

You get zero for being here. You gain everything when you explore and enjoy the experiences you are having regardless of your judgment of what goes on but there is no reward for doing a good job here.

As always, this is a choice only the individual can make.

Can you stop and listen to your heart?

Can you understand you are here to experience all this life has to offer?

Can you stop judging the experiences that you have?

What are you going to choose to do?

Angel Amy

Additional Articles

When you wake up in the middle of the night...

We have been told by society that we need 8 hours of sleep every day. If you want to break free from what society has taught you, all you have to do is change the story.

Instead of beating yourself up and asking why can't you sleep start telling yourself something new? Begin to tell yourself the reason you are not sleeping is because your guidance team is working on you, energetically.

When you are awake you are conscious. When you are conscious you are able to integrate. When you integrate you are allowing changes within your body to take place. You are being worked on and upgraded during your sleep time.

When you sleep you cannot integrate the work that is being done on yourself. This is why you wake up in the middle of the night. You are being worked on and you need to integrate the work that is being done.

Your team does not operate from a place of time. They don't care what time they work on you, all they know is they need to work on you and sometimes that interferes with your sleep.

Sometimes that is why you feel exhausted during the day and feel the need to take a nap, it's because your team needs to work on you. If you honor what you feel and are able to take a nap begin to tell your team that you are ready for the work.

The next time you wake up in the middle of the night tell yourself you are allowing the integration of the work they have just done.

When the mind gets out of the way and you trust that you are being worked on by your team you will wake up in the morning and feel as if you got your so called 8 hours of sleep. You will not feel as if you lost any sleep. Your team knows what they are doing.

As always this is a choice only you can make.

Are you going to continue to beat yourself up when you wake up in the middle of the night?

Are you going to allow your team to do the work on you and wake up fully refreshed?

What are you going to choose?

Angel Amy

You can't take it with you

Usually this phrase gets brought up in regards to money. We often say that you can't take your money with you when you die.

The real meaning of this is not that you can't take your money with you, which is also true, it is more about not taking your fears and negativity with you as you move forward into the new energy.

You cannot walk forward into the new levels carrying your fears, judgments, doubts or any form of unworthiness with you.

This is the junk that you cannot bring forward with you. This is the junk that needs to be released.

There is no right, wrong, good or bad when you decide what it is that you will choose to do. All choices are always valid and all choices lead forward. The speed at which you move forward is determined by the choices you make.

Start to listen with your heart and not your head.

You cannot take it with you.

You cannot take any form of negativity or unworthiness with you. It just won't work where we are going.

As always the choice is yours to make.

What are you going to choose to do?

Angel Amy

One of the keys to life is to understand that this reality we are living in is a game. If you cannot get that understanding life will continue to be hard for you. When you understand this concept you will be more able to navigate your way through it. You can either play the game or the game will play you.

Acknowledgment

Here are just a few people I would like to thank that have helped me on my journey. The ones mentioned have been an extremely important part of my journey and they all came into my life in a very magical way.

Some of these people I have never met but they among others have helped to support me through my awakening journey here.

I would like to thank my sister Jill Pierce for introducing me to the spirit world. I want to thank her for all her encouragement and support to get me to where I now am. She has been by my side ever since I began my path of awakening. I cannot say enough about how she has helped me get to where I am today. I could not have done it without her and I am truly blessed that she is my sister.

My work began with the help of the following people. They have encouraged me in many ways and I thank them for their friendship on this journey of mine.

Elvia Roe of AngelsTeach.com
Peter Roe of LoveYourHumanDesign.com
Dawn Simpson of AngelDawning.com
Michael Tatlock of Michaeltatlockcoaching.com
Nick Dellacava of TeamOfLightCommunications.com
Debra DeWees whom I have had the pleasure of meeting only once.

There are many others who have been there for me.

I would like to thank my family and all my friends who have been there on this journey with me. My family always supported my Angel work even though most of them did not fully understand what I was doing.

The friends I have are few but they are quality friends and they too have always supported my Angel work and I thank everyone who has known me.

Some of my best supporters are people who I have met online as clients that have become friends and to this day I have never met them in person but they feel like family now.

I would like to thank my Mom and Dad, brother Gerry, Baby Girl, Grandma and Grandpa and Uncle Dana who have passed on and who I believe are helping me from the other side. I have seen physical signs of their presence and find it truly magical.

My family consist of 5 living brothers and 5 living sisters.

Nick who is married to Renee, Greg who is married to Maria, John who is married to Danelle, Theresa, Paul who is married to Jodi, Tom who is married to Jenn, Trisha, Cilla who is married to Peter and my little sister Jill.

I am truly grateful to have my son Shaun, my granddaughter Holly, who has given me the Slogan *'I can tow you out of your misery'*, to my great grandchildren Aubri and Lincoln, as well as to my nieces and nephews. Thank you for all of your love!

I would like to thank everyone for the love and support I needed in order to continue on this Angel path of mine and I look forward to writing my next book.

Printed in the United States
By Bookmasters